T0065438

A GARDEN

of

Poetry

Come Stroll With Me Through
My Garden of Poetry

JEANETTE POLE WATTLEY

BALBOA.PRESS

A DIVISION OF HAY HOUSE

Balboa Press books may be ordered through booksellers or by contacting:

Balboa Press
A Division of Hay House
1663 Liberty Drive
Bloomington, IN 47403
www.balboapress.com
844-682-1282

Print information available on the last page.

ISBN: 978-1-9822-5248-9 (sc)
ISBN: 978-1-9822-5249-6 (e)

Balboa Press rev. date: 11/28/2020

Contents

Friendship & Love

Inspirational Reflections

Life Lessons and it's Seasons

Our Country and it's Politics

Religion as a Relationship

Acknowledgements

This book has been a long time in the making, but it is finally a reality!

First of all, I want to thank God, for allowing me the privilege to accomplish this great task, and giving me everything that I needed to get it done!

Next, I would like to thank my husband, Desmond Wattley, Sr. for all the help that he provided me during the process." Keeping track of all of those computer files and folders were no easy task, but you made it seem like child's play." "I couldn't have done it without you, my love!"

I would also like to thank my children: Desmond, Jr. (now deceased), Donna, Curtis and Rahmel. I wouldn't have done it without your encouragement, and constantly pushing me to. Lots of my inspiration for writing, came from the many things that I learned while raising you all.

To my Mom and Dad, Arnold and Rita Pole, now deceased. They never stopped encouraging me to get my poetry published, so, I know they would be overjoyed by this accomplishment!

To my brothers, Alden Pole and Glen Pole; and to my sister Ingrid Pole Hutchinson. You all never stopped encouraging me, to get my poetry published.

Alden, you even made me a beautiful cover for the folder where I keep my poetry. I believe that started the feeling of knowing that I needed to get it done.

Glen, you always invited me to read my poetry at all of those 'special' events that you held at your home...I guess it was so everybody would be asking me, when I was going to publish my poetry.

Ingrid, you went as far as threatening never to speak with me again, if I didn't get it done...and you know I couldn't have that!

Finally, to all my other family, and friends who never stopped, believing in me! Every time I would write you a 'special' poem, you would ask, when was I going to get my work out there...well, here it is!

Dedication

This book is dedicated to the memory of our first-born son, Desmond Llewelyn Wattley, Jr.

I am thankful for all the experiences that he brought into my life; they inspired me to write many of the poetry in this book. He will 'forever' be remembered, and 'always' missed.

Friendship & Love

Let's take a stroll...

A Mother's Love

Mother, I love you, words seldom said, but true,
I wouldn't be here today, if it wasn't for you.
You carried me nine months, kept me safe and secure,
and when I finally got here, you loved me some more.

You've been a real blessing in my life I must say,
though sometimes, as a youngster, I didn't see it that way.
I remember the times when I tried to rebel;
at times I disappointed you, I could tell.

Your teachings and warnings I often resisted,
but I'm glad despite "me", you continually persisted.
Your standards for us, as your children, were high;
I remember sometimes I would sit down and cry!

But now looking back over years that's gone by,
I thank you for your strong-will, and that is no lie!
It's made me the person that I am today,
not perfect, but trying to get there day by day.

You should be proud mother; you raised us up right!
Thank God for His guidance, direction, and light!
As I look at my children all grown up today,
I think about you, and the part you did play.

I know you weren't here with them every day,
but I could hear your voice, when to them I would say;
"That's not right, don't do it that way", or,
"What goes around comes around, sure as the day!"

Yes, things that you taught me, I passed on to them,
and I hope that as parents, they will do that as well.
As we pass these high standards from one to the next,
this family that started with Dad and you, will be blessed!

A Woman's Love

The essence of a woman, is more than you behold!
On the outside, you see the curves
and feel the warmth of her flesh,
but the inner parts, the soul,
is much more complex than you can digest.
It is what makes her a woman!
The depths of her soul, feelings untold,
the hurt, the pain of all the years.
Behold a person, a whole being,
needing to be loved, with a love that
only you can unfold!

It is no easy task to love a woman;
it takes a love undying, faithful, true,
one that will never wander, or wonder why you?
A love that never falters, never fails,
but stands up to the test and yet prevails.
It takes a man of honor and of patience,
to love a woman to the very end,
and when you've given all you feel you can give;
something's gone wrong and there we go again.

Yes, there we go again, her feelings hurt,
and what's it worth?
She stands, head hanging low in pain,
not caring to discuss but to refrain.
It hurts. Don't sleep on it,
cause, life won't be the same if you don't quit.
She may act unaware that things aren't great,
but just believe me, it's the fights she hate.
Don't mean that she's not going to discuss it,
it only means that you'll just have to wait.

Don't be confused, no you didn't fool her;
she just refuses to let your games control her.
Cause, it's been said, and I do agree,
"what goes around will come around", you'll see.
Yes, when at last you go the final round,
and all the hurtful things been said and done;
just look and see who is left standing,
and look and see who is on the ground.
Yes, you've just lost your woman's love!

Call to Friendship

I call you friend; you've always been there for me.
I call you friend, in all sincerity.
I call you friend, when I am sad and lonely.
I call you friend; the best in me you see.

I call you friend; you've never tried to hurt me.
I call you friend; I trust you, totally.
I call you friend; my secrets you hold dearly.
I call you friend; I mean it sincerely!

You call me friend; I'm all that you've been to me.
You call me friend; we feel it mutually.
You call me friend, because you truly trust me.
You call me friend; your friend I'll always be.

You call me friend; yes, you are patient with me.
You call me friend; my faults you do not see.
You call me friend, you see special things about me.
You call me friend, though others sometimes disagree.

Yes, we are friends; we have a special friendship,
a bond that nothing, or no one can destroy.
We will not let anything come between us,
for we are friends, a 'special' friendship we enjoy!

Dear Friend

My dear friend, though we must now part,
you'll always hold a special place in my heart.
I may not see you as often, it's true,
but just remember, "I'll always be there for you."

You have been a wonderful friend I must say;
you were patient when I didn't see things your way.
You wished me well with the choices I made,
and for many of them, a 'dear' price I have paid.

But you stood by me; you didn't desert me,
you waited to see what the outcome would be.
You reassured me, and by me you stood,
whether it turned out to be bad or good.

So dear friend as we go our separate ways,
may your life be blessed with many good days.
I'll never forsake you in good times or in bad,
cause, you are the best friend that I ever had!

Every Time

Every time I try to make things right, something goes wrong.
Every time I tell myself, you must be strong.
There's something blocking all of the positives,
and trying to make us focus on the negatives.

I must be "Me"; I must keep reaching for the sky.

There's no one there to pick me up, if I should fall.
Yes, I am scared, for I have given it my all!
At times I feel I did what needed be done;
then there're times I feel, the task I should have shunned.

What is it, what is it that's expected of me?
Must I just live and not be who I want to be?
Must I just sit like a treasure on a shelf,
and be an ornament or anything, except myself?

My soul says no; there is too much at stake!
Why sit around and do nothing, but wait?
No one seems to have my interest, anyhow,
so, I'll do what I need to, and get by somehow!

If someone cares, and this you must remember,
you being yourself, should not bring them to anger.
To hear you speak should make them proud to know you;
they should be happy with you being you.

They will enjoy each moment they spend with you.
They'll cherish everything you say and do.
They'll stand behind you and they'll push you each day,
while making sure you're not an easy prey.

When others criticize you, they'll defend you,
and not find reasons to attack you, too.
They'll overlook the bad and see the good,
when by others you are misunderstood.

Friends to Lovers

They met and right away they knew,
that friends they'd want to be,
and as they talked it was so clear,
they felt it mutually!

They had a lot in common;
ambitions, hopes and dreams.
They talked and talked for hours,
at least that's how it seems.

And as the weeks and months went by,
their friendship did not end,
they stood together through thick and thin,
and they became good friends.

Then one day things began to change,
seems they had turned a bend;
both realizing they were falling,
for the one they had called "friend"!

They wondered how much things would change,
would this be where it ends?
Oh yes, things changed, but through it all,
they still remained good friends!

And as their feelings grew and grew,
and as they fell in love;
they realized; they'd found 'that one',
thank their lucky stars above!

From friends to lovers, some folks say,
don't ever go that way;
it could be a big mistake, they say,
you'll be sorry for that day!

I'm sure there're those who will disagree,
you'll have to take that chance and see.
but of this I'm sure, 'all' will agree,
"what's meant to be, will be"!

Friends

I was sinking, sinking low;
you grabbed my hand and would not let go.
"I'm here for you," said a soft sweet voice,
just remember, you do have a choice."

You can decide to fall apart,
and probably die of a broken heart.
You can decide to stand and fight,
with everything in you that's right!

You can decide to hang in there,
although the outcome is not clear.
And on the other hand, I know,
you can decide to just let go.

You make your choice, I'm still your friend,
I will be with you to the end.
But after all is said and done,
what will I do if my friend is gone?

Friendship

A friend is one who loves you, no matter what you do;
they'll tell you if you are wrong, but the friendship will be true.
I have friends that I treasure, because they are so neat,
the friendship just gets better, each and every time we meet!

Love for a Lifetime

Life takes us to that certain place, that makes us wonder, why?
It then brings us to a place, with someone 'special' by our side.
Life truly is a wonder! We continually marvel how,
two people meet and fall in love, beneath the stars above!

There is that magic moment so splendid and so grand,
that brings us to that time and place, we'll never understand!
Love brings a special feeling, so grandeur and so fine,
I pray that when you find that love, it will last a lifetime!

Love of Family and Friends

Family and friends are like rays of light, that God puts in our life;
they brighten our path along the way, they're there to give us light.
The things they do, the words they speak, lights up the part we walk;
they give us strength, and helps us, not to stumble in the dark.
We should not take for granted all the kindness that they show;
the words of love and the good deeds, that help to make us grow.
And so, with all sincerity, and from the bottom of our hearts;
we should be very thankful for the love that they impart!

Love

Love, oh that feeling unsurpassed by any other,
it takes you high and brings you low,
sometimes it makes you shudder!
It sparks the flame, ignites the soul,
sometimes it makes you loose control!
But, oh, the beauty of it all,
is no one thinks before they fall!

Love makes you laugh, and it makes you cry,
sometimes you may feel you want to die.
Oh, give it time, and you will see;
if it is really meant to be.
There will be good times, there will be bad.
There'll be happy times as well as sad.
But, don't despair, true love will last;
so, don't you worry, this too shall pass!

And when your love has passed the test,
and when you feel now, we can rest,
don't be surprised if more tests come,
to try and break your 'love-thing' down!
Just pull some strength out of the past,
cause, now you know, your love will last!

My Friend

My friend you are so special, you mean the world to me;
you've always been there for me, when I needed company.
Through good times and hard times, through failure and success,
you've been a friend that I could trust, my friend you are the best!

From you I learned so many things, some of which you're not aware;
I learned to respect others, though their opinions I may not share.
I learned to choose my battles, and fight them carefully;
I learned that we could simply, agree to disagree.

We've had our disagreements and our compromises too.
We've had our share of battles, I lost some, and so did you.
But through it all we learned one thing that's very, very clear;
true friendship will endure through many storms, and still be there!

I'll always be there for you, whatever paths our lives may take;
this bond will not be broken, and that is no mistake!
I will always be a friend to you, one on whom you can depend;
don't hesitate to call me, should you ever need a friend.

And as I write these words to you, and the tears begin to fall,
it would take another lifetime for me to say it all.
There is so much I want to say, mere words cannot express,
so, let me end by wishing you, God's love and happiness!

Remember When

The day that you moved in next door,
I knew I had a friend for sure!
We were both young and carefree then,
but now we can remember when.

Remember your first day at school,
some of your classmates were so cruel?
When it was time to go out and play,
they looked at you and turned away?

Remember when, throughout the years,
we laughed and cried and shed some tears?
Remember when we both left home;
how we felt oh, so all alone?

Remember on your wedding day,
how much I cried but you could not stay?
We vowed that we would stay in touch,
but I still missed you oh, so much!

Remember when I called and said,
that both my mom and dad were dead?
I had no desire to go on,
but you told me I must be strong.

Remember when I called real late,
to let you know I'd had a date?
It was the beginning of my new life,
he soon asked me to be his wife!

And then, of course, the children came,
and we were there for each other again.
We shared the joys that children bring;
oh, it was such a joyous thing!

And as the years go by so fast,
as the present and future become the past,
you will always be my life-long friend,
we'll grow old and gray and remember when!

The Friendship Chain

The links are strong, the chain is thick,
it's hard to break the friendship clique.
Friends are a group that's tossed together,
and yes, they do support each other!

Through thick and thin they do not budge,
they defend each other, they do not judge.
And if by chance, one of them fall,
a helping hand is lent by all.

They do not judge, they just support.
They do not believe the bad report.
Yes, friendship is a bond you see,
that surpasses many a mystery!

The Friendship Test

Friendship has that special bond,
there's no other way to view it.
Cause you will find that in the end,
the testing will reveal it.

To have a friend, you must be a friend,
there's no ands and buts about it.
If you find you cannot be that friend,
you may as well forget it.

Don't try pretending to be a friend,
if you're really not into it.
Time will tell, you just rest assured,
the 'test' will truly prove it.

In every friendship there comes a time,
something will come to test it.
Will you be that fair-weather friend,
or will your friendship pass it?

The only way you'll truly know,
is if your friendship can outlast it.
So, here's the question I'll like to pose…
Will your friendship really pass it?

Wedding Bliss

Please say no, it ain't so, say there's more to it than this!
For if this is it, then I can't see, why they call it wedding bliss!

You find your perfect partner, there's no one else for sure,
no matter how they beg or plead, or come knocking on your door.
You stop all that you're doing, by, and for yourself that is.
You try your very best to meet, not your own needs, but his.

And then you think you've had it, the perfect wedding day.
The day that each girl longs for, and hope and wait and pray.
And now that all that's over, you ask, "what did I miss?"
You feel so sad and lonely, and they call it wedding bliss?

This cry comes from a young girl, who in her rush to grow,
thought that she would get married, but little did she know.
She did not ask for guidance, she did not seek advice.
She did not wait to hear from God, so now she'll pay the price.

Oh, yes, she thought she knew it all, she knew it must be love,
but love does not come easy, it is sent from up above.
Love takes some time to get here, it spends some time in flight;
and that is why I don't believe in true love at first sight!

Oh yes, there's an attraction, that knocks you off your feet;
sometimes it sends you spinning, when that 'special' one you meet.
That's why you need to take the time, to learn if it is true;
never accept the 'baggage', soon as it gets to you.

I know it's not a nice term, but I also know it's true;
we all come with some baggage, in all sizes, old, and new.
So, before you make the wedding plans, some sorting you must do;
you must sort out the baggage, and what you keep is up to you.

Yes, marriage is a commitment, that involves, oh, so much,
so, choosing the right partner, creates that perfect touch.
And even though sometimes, you may not have much money,
you can be a happy 'queen' bee, with lots and lots of honey!

There'll be less disappointments, if you choose carefully,
you can go on and live your life, as a happy family!
There'll be no need for you, to wonder what you missed,
because you will be living, in 'perfect' wedding bliss!

Wedding Day

Two hearts, today are made one, as they unite in love;
and they are being showered, with blessings from above.
The heavenly Father saw it fit, to join these two together;
to form a very special bond that shall never, never sever.

So, as the organ plays the beautiful wedding song,
the flower girls walk down the aisles, the walk seems oh so long!
The bridesmaids follow close behind; then the Maid of Honor;
and finally enters the beautiful bride, dressed in all her splendor!

The ceremony then begins and vows are soon exchanged;
the groom can't wait to kiss his bride, as he looks into her face!
The beauty of the moment, the love that runs so deep;
tears of joy that's shed by many, will make a strong man weep!

The families and friends all share in this blessed event;
there are lots of food and music; lots of good wishes sent.
The cake is cut, the bouquet is thrown, and so is the garter belt;
everyone rushed to take part, not matter how they felt!

This very special occasion will be remembered by all,
but most of all the bride and groom, as they rush to leave the hall!
A shiny limo's waiting, to whisk them on their honeymoon.
Yes, they will soon be all alone in their own 'private' room!

As they start on their new life; as they begin their family;
they'll love each other as promised, yes, everyone will see!
And as they love each other, as they go along life's way;
they'll never forget the vows they made, on their wedding day!

Why

Why would you love someone, who shows you in every way;
that their love for you just isn't there, no matter what they say?
Love is not trying so very hard, just to avoid each other.
Love is sharing, love is caring, and doing things together.

There will be times when you will each require your own space,
but it should not be very long, till you come face to face.
Since love is an attraction, that draws two hearts together,
you will soon feel, within your hearts, a longing for each other.

The things that make you happy, from doing he refrains,
but he always seems to want to do the things that cause you pain.
She always seems to want to do the things that make you sad,
but she never seems to want do the things that make you glad.

No, that's not love, let's try again, where is the caring there?
If it was love, feelings would show, it would be very clear!
So why, you ask, do you go on believing it's all-good?
Because, sometimes, it hurts to know, that we misunderstood!

Some interesting thoughts...

Inspirational Reflections

A Child's Pain

The little girl sat quiet, as quiet as a mouse,
while the other children ran, and played throughout the house.
For in her heart she knew, injustice had been done,
so, she sat there like the cat, just done stole her tongue.
She would go on day after day, living with the pain,
of that dark secret hidden, inside her little frame.

She lives in fear not knowing when the monster would return,
and she'll be forced to summit, willingly, to his call.
She had no choice she thought, yes; she knew that it was wrong,
but how could she fight someone so very big and strong?
Deep inside her little soul, she felt she would explode;
so sad that such a little girl, must carrying this heavy load.

So, day by day and night by night, she lives with so much fear,
not knowing just how much more, she would have to bear.
If only someone would just stop, and look at her more closely,
they would see a woman living where a child once used to be.
Cause someone came into her life, and took the liberty,
and stole from that dear little child, her innocence and purity.

No, Momma must not know, the pain she must not show;
yet, she hopes someone would notice that she was hurting, though.
But how would that occur? What is she waiting for?
Yes, someone came and took her childhood joy away from her!
In its place they left a lonely child who may never know,
just where to start to heal the pain, for the scars will never show!

A Flower

A flower blooms for a while and then it fades away;
gone is that fragrance oh so sweet, the brightened up your day.
The beauty of those petals, made perfect by God's hands;
The many colors, many sizes, all fitting in His plans.
Some grow in someone's garden; some grow along the paths;
no matter where we find them, they always touch our hearts.
Imagine for a moment, though, that the flowers got no rain,
they'd wither up, so quickly, oh that would be a shame!
Those beautiful flowers, so pretty, would last for a short time,
but they would never flourish like the ones that got sunshine.
Our lives are like the flowers, a beauty to behold,
but if not 'nourished' it will produce, many sad tales untold!

Any Day Now

Any day now! What, do you really expect me to believe?
Yes, there's that possibility to perceive that things will change,
but, with that change in mind we set the stage for future rage.
Cause, when "any day now" do not come at last,
we cannot understand why it has not come to pass.

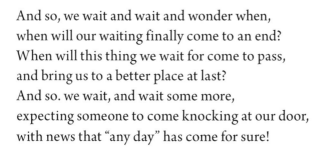

And so, we try to make some sense of it,
but there's no sense in promises unfulfilled!
We wonder still, why we were made to hope,
and in this whole mentality, we missed the boat;
the one that may have taken us where we long to be.
And so, the answer still remains a mystery!

And so, we wait and wait and wonder when,
when will our waiting finally come to an end?
When will this thing we wait for come to pass,
and bring us to a better place at last?
And so. we wait, and wait some more,
expecting someone to come knocking at our door,
with news that "any day" has come for sure!

Any day, any one, any time, sounds all the same.
They are words that do not give a true time-frame.
Any, is a small word vague in meaning.
It is not specific and sometimes so deceiving.
It promises something, but what, is not quite clear.
It makes one stop and wonder if the promise is sincere.

So, finally it's time for analyzing.
Must you keep waiting, or stop fantasizing?
Should you wake up to a new reality,
admitting what you want may never be?
Should you at least accept, responsibility,
to make the change you seek, a possibly?

Do what you must! Sometimes it is up to us,
to make the change, that get us where we want to be.
And so, the search continues for reality.
Yes, **any day now,** we may hear well-done, and take a bow!

Black Brother

Tall black brother,
handsome black brother,
walking like you own the world black brother!
Short black brother,
average black brother,
educated and self-educated black brother.
Can you educate another black brother?

Successful black brother,
resourceful black brother;
have you given back to your younger black brother?
Articulate black brother,
street-smart black brother;
look around and you'll see a hurting black brother.

Caring black brother,
loving black brother;
take care of your seed, they need you, black brother!
Crying black brother,
dying black brother;
not using protection can kill you, black brother!

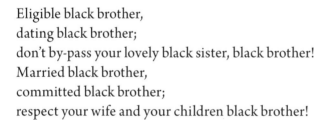

Eligible black brother,
dating black brother;
don't by-pass your lovely black sister, black brother!
Married black brother,
committed black brother;
respect your wife and your children black brother!

Godly black brother,
humble black brother;
let God have control of your life black brother!
Happy black brother,
fulfilled black brother,
you'll find this in doing God's will black brother!

Blow Breeze Blow

The breeze is so refreshing; it touches the very soul;
it stimulates the body, and seems to make you whole!
It brushes soft against the skin, like water in a cup;
so soothing and refreshing; it makes the mind wake up!

The constant motion of the leaves, like rhythm to a dance;
like music playing in the air, they swing and sway and prance.
Yes, in their every motion, there's a lesson to be learned;
a lesson of tranquility, that comes from up above!

So, blow breeze blow, keep blowing, so hard against my flesh;
continue breeze to soothe me, and my whole-body refresh!
Blow stronger, stronger till I find,
yes, breeze, 'You' blow my mind!"

Crying

Crying brings such great relief, from all the hurt and pain;
it's a good way of releasing stress, so don't you be ashamed.
You can cry all you want too, let the tears flow down your face,
but when you're finished crying, just stand up and take your place!

After crying comes the action! What are you going to do?
You must decide to handle it, or it will handle you.
Are you just going to sit around and wallow in your tears,
or will you stand up strong and tall, in spite of all your fears?

And then there are the tears of joy, the ones you can't control,
those too are very special, from deep within the soul!
You see them shed at weddings, and at birthdays too.
You see them when your baby takes that first step towards you!

Yes, there is a season for everything; the Bible makes it clear,
a time to laugh, a time to cry, but please do not despair!
The Bible also tells us, and for this we are all yearning,
weeping may endure for a night, but joy comes in the morning!

Fossils

Fossils are the remains of dinosaurs and such;
people search for, and collect them, yes, you can find so much.
There are many, many species; there are many, many types;
if you like collecting fossils, you can find the ones you like.

I've never searched for fossils, but I might one of these days;
they are something that interests me, in so many, many ways.
Just thinking of the dinosaurs that walked the earth before,
makes me want to read and learn, about them even more!

So, learning about fossils, is what I'm going to do,
then one day I may break away, and find some fossils too!
Yes, fossils are exciting, for in them lies the past;
so people will always collect them, as long as this world lasts!

In Flight

Yes, I went there, and I have just returned.
You ask me, where, but need I say right now?
I roam about this land in all its splendor,
and oh, so often I do stop and wonder!

Does it sound easy? Oh, it's very easy,
not caring that I sound like I am crazy.
I travel distant lands from day to day,
and visit places that are far away.

It cost me nothing to explore the planet;
my heart perceives it, and I go right for it.
I visit places I have never been before,
knowing that they will open every door!

If you desire to reach your full potential,
then, you, too, have what is so essential.
Just grab your "mind" and then just set it free…
yes, it will take you where you want to be!

Looking Back

As I look back and reminisce on younger days gone by,
the years flew by so swiftly, like the clouds up in the sky.
In all the turmoil of those days, if I have one regret,
It would have to be the "focus" that my children did not get.

I spent too much time trying to change things I could not,
instead of investing more time in the precious gifts I got.
The gifts of my four children, who mean the world to me,
the gift of God's own precious son, who died to set me free!

I know I cannot change what's done, but for what it's worth,
there's nothing else more precious, than the ones you've given birth!
I tried to be a good mom; I did the best I could,
but sometimes I did put myself, before the greater good.

For that I'm truly sorry, I would change it if I could,
but mistakes are a part of life, and that is understood.
And so, for the mistakes I've made, for which I've been forgiven;
I learned a lesson from each one, and I'm on my way to heaven!

Me

I! Me! Woman of the world,
I have arrived and, yes, myself I do applaud!
You ask me do tell how I came to this conclusion?
No, I'm not wrong, and this is no illusion!

My beginnings, well, they were very humble.
in fact, if you didn't watch it, you may stumble.
So, let me take you back to where I came from,
and walk you through the makings of a small town.

Yes, though from humble beginnings I do hail,
my family worked so very hard to pave the trail.
It was no easy task, to this I must confess,
but with God's help, our family passed the test!

My dad, a man of steel who ruled his household well,
was not one to be fooled with, that we all could tell!
Yet, even though sometimes he could be very tough,
we also knew that he loved his family very much.

My mom a woman we could count on to console,
would stand up for us like an open parasol.
In times of thunder showers and non-stop rain,
she somehow managed to sooth the growing pains.

And then one day I walked away all grown-up,
about to face the world and drink from my own cup.
Yes, that I did! I went and drank it all up,
oh yes, and on this life, I really did sup!

Sometimes it got real tough, but did I quit?
No, anything's worth having is worth the wait!
I licked my wounds and, yes, I stuck with it,
now, I've arrived, though I may be a little late.

I know that it's only for little while,
then, I'll smile, toss it aside and leave with pride.
Until then, though, I'll take life stride by stride,
cause, it's not over till we reach the other side.

We all must work until God says we've had it,
cause it's not over till it's over, and we know it.
I'll always strive to be the best I can be,
then pass the torch on to the ones behind me!

Mountains and Valleys

Mountains high, valleys low, where do you want to go?
They each will serve a purpose as you walk through life, you know.
There are lessons to be learned sitting on the mountaintop,
and yet the lessons that we learn in the valleys, never stop.

Let's take a quick look at it, and see if this is true;
in order to reach the mountain, the valley we must pass through.
And when at last we get close to that gorgeous mountain hue,
the journey has just started, as the mountaintop we view.

In fact, we must be rested, before we start the climb,
that's what the valley is for, with its low planes and inclines.
As we wander through the valley, we eat and we are fed;
we need our strength for climbing that mountain up ahead.

In the valley there are lots of folks, just trying to survive;
some will never climb the mountain or see the other side.
They are contented just to stay, in the valley all lifelong;
yet who are we to judge them, and say that they are wrong?

Cause, as we walk through the valley, we need them for support;
though they never leave the valley, they can surely help us cope.
So, as you near the mountain, don't look back at them and sneer,
just thank them for the knowledge you gained while you were there.

As up the mountain you proceed, yes, inch-by-inch you climb,
take each lesson that you learned, and walk up the mountainside.
Then when at last you reach the top, and the valley you survey,
don't forget you may need their help, as you come down one day!

Ms. Every 'Thang'

Ms. Every 'Thang', our perfect one, works very hard each day;
she's in by 9 and out by 5, but stays when she needs to stay.
She's patient, loyal, caring, she's understanding too;
she knows her job quite well, and does what she needs to do.

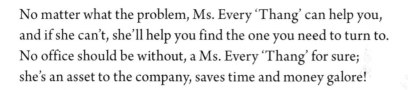

Dependable, loyal, and competent as well!
Respectful, and committed, that everyone can tell.
Such an outstanding person, Ms. Every 'Thang' she is;
her colleagues will all tell you, she really knows her biz...

She's respectful, and she's focused; she's competent as hell,
her colleague will also tell you, she's dependable as well!
Ms. Every 'Thang', she is a 'must' for employee relations;
every time you look around, someone's coming to her station.

No matter what the problem, Ms. Every 'Thang' can help you,
and if she can't, she'll help you find the one you need to turn to.
No office should be without, a Ms. Every 'Thang' for sure;
she's an asset to the company, saves time and money galore!

My Baby

I felt a little flutter, and at first, I could not utter;
then I tried again to mutter, but it turned in to a stutter.
I tried to express the joy I felt that God had chosen me,
to bring a child into the world, what a blessing that would be!
To bless me with a baby, that God Himself would choose,
and just to know that I would be, the vessel He would use!

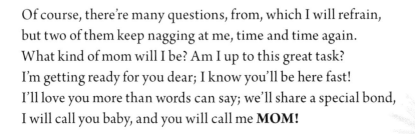

Yes, God has chosen to use me, to bring a child to earth,
and with great appreciation we anticipate the birth!
And as the days and weeks go by, yes, everyone can see,
that I will soon become a mom, what joy that brings to me!
Yes, as I sit, I think about the responsibility;
I know it will be up to me to raise you properly.

Of course, there're many questions, from, which I will refrain,
but two of them keep nagging at me, time and time again.
What kind of mom will I be? Am I up to this great task?
I'm getting ready for you dear; I know you'll be here fast!
I'll love you more than words can say; we'll share a special bond,
I will call you baby, and you will call me **MOM!**

My Daddy

Tall and handsome, that's how he stood,
turning heads of every woman who walked by.
"That's my daddy", I remember thinking,
even though sometimes I felt a little slighted.

He was around but, oh, so hard to find!
The days would come and go and no daddy would I see.
I know he loved me, but was he devoted to me,
or did those glancing ladies occupy his world,
leaving no attention for "daddy's little girl?"

I missed him, oh how I missed him!
Yet, I never doubted his love for me.

We grew apart; he broke my heart, by never trying to
understand that longing for his presence in my life.
Then I grew up, and daddy still wasn't there;
he moved on and got himself another wife.

But I still loved my daddy with an undying love!
So, now he's old, he's lived a long life; he's been truly blessed!
I go and see him and as we talk and reminisce,
I wonder if he knows, just how much he 'really' missed!

Oh Island!

Oh Island, sweet island, known as the Virgin Isle;
over the years they've come, and taken away your smile.
They took away your innocence, oh where did it go?
It hurts to see what they have done, to my island, I love so!

They did not treat you right my dear, I see tears in your eyes.
It makes me sad to see this, oh beautiful Virgin Isle!
In years gone by, you were the best, but one by one they came;
they took all that you had to give, and that is such a shame!

Oh Island, sweet Island, still you continue to provide,
a place where I can come to, a beauty so divine.
Yes, in the outer parts of you there's still beauty to behold,
but time has really hurt your inner beauty; your inner soul!

You served us well, you stood the test; you've been there for us all,
and that is why Dear Island, we will not let you fall.
We'll work hard to redeem you, as a people we'll stand strong!
Oh Island, sweet Island, for the days gone by we long!

We long to see that beauty which once was yours divine!
We long to feel the pride we had in you dear Virgin Isle!
We long for the high standards you held as a great place!
Oh Island, sweet Island, we long for those good old days!

You may not have been experienced in many ways of the world,
but you sure did make us happy, and for that we do applaud!
Though you may have to struggle, the lost things to regain;
oh island, sweet island, you'll fly high once again!

Past Due

The book comes from the library, with a date that it is due.
The card on back will let me know, just what you need to do.
The milk comes with a date stamped clearly on the cartoon,
and if that date is passed, the milk you won't consume.

The can food has a stamped date, to tell us if it's fresh,
and if the date has passed, with that food we do not mess!
We need to be reminded, whenever things are due,
I need to be reminded, and people so do you.

What in your life is past due, what do you need to do?
Send flowers to a love one, or call to say, "How are you?"
Don't let these things go undone there's always a price to pay;
so before they become "Pass Due", let's do these things today!

Reading

Reading is a great way, to learn things we do not know.
It is a tool to help us, if we really want to grow.
It helps build understanding; it helps build self-esteem.
Yes, reading helps us in many ways, as students to succeed!

Reading is Fundamental

Reading is fundamental, it accomplishes many tasks;
it tells us of the future, yet does not neglect the past.
Just think of all the things you'll miss, if only you could not read.
You'll miss the signs along the way, with their messages to heed.
You'll miss out on the letters that a friend could write to you.
You'll miss out on so many things, that reading makes come true.
Yes, all the great adventures, to lands both far and near;
if you could find it in a book, you could imagine you were there!

Reading just for Fun

Through reading I've discovered, so many things I did not know;
I can also visit places, where I may never go.
There is nothing quite like reading, it captures body, mind and soul;
it takes us to the future, and shows us what it holds.
It also tells us of the past, and shows us how far we've come.
Yes, reading is a great thing; it can be so much fun!

Procrastination

Procrastination is a thief; he'll steal your time away!
You wake up thinking, "There is something I must do today",
but as the day goes by, you just push it aside;
and then before you know it, oops, here comes the evening tide!

"Tomorrow I will do it", that's what you tell yourself,
but you are only fooling, you and no one else.
Cause, when tomorrow gets here, other things will cloud your mind;
so, what you had to do today, you'll do it another time.

And so, the days they come and go, some things get done it's true,
but did you ever do that thing, that you set out to do?
Oh no, it never happened, so now you know it's true;
procrastination came by, and stole that thought from you!

Procrastination is a thief, I guess I proved my case,
so, you should always try your best to keep him on the chase!
When you see him coming, for a visit to your place,
just run and do what you need to; he will leave you in a haste!

Rain

The storm clouds gather in the sky,
and we sit around and wonder, why
a sunny day has turned to rain,
and it has brought us so much pain.

But friend, don't shake your head and frown,
thank God for the tap…tap…on the ground!
For without rain, there'll be no trees,
and no leaves blowing in the breeze.

In spring the flowers won't bloom so pretty,
and that will be oh such a pity!
No April showers to make them grow,
after the long cold winter's snow.

We won't have the water that we drink.
What will we do, I don't want to think?
Yes, water is the staff of life,
so, welcome the rain into your life!

So, next time the rain falls in your life,
don't sit around and wonder, why?
Open your arms, embrace the rain;
and you will grow, despite the pain!

School's Back In

School's back in, there are other lessons to be learned.
I know you thought, your degree you had earned,
but don't you know my students, that learning never ceases?
So, here we go again, hoping your knowledge soon increases!

The first lesson I want to teach, is one you must address,
just study hard and do your best and you will pass each test.
You must be quiet and let me teach, if you really want to learn;
of course, if there are questions, you will surely get your turn.

As long as there is the breath of life flowing through your body,
there will be opportunities to open your mind and study.
I know you graduated, and you were congratulated,
but now you're back in school again, and I hope you are elated!

Open the door, sit down, relax, cause you've been here before,
I know you learned your lesson well, but now I have some more!
I know you're a little nervous, I can tell from your expression,
but don't let it overwhelm you, it's just another session!

Some things to reflect on ...

School

School is a place for learning and making new friends too.
You will learn things to help you, in everything you do.
The work may seem hard sometimes, lots of homework to complete,
but it will help you when you're grown, and for a job you must compete.

Sisters

Sisters are special people, though sometimes you may disagree,
but when you need someone to talk to, your sister it will be.
They are always there to listen, and lend a helping hand;
sisters are very special; this you must understand.

Trees

I have an evergreen tree right outside my window pane,
I see it when it's sunny; I see it when it rains.
Throughout the year it is green, springtime showers make it grow;
though it is green in winter, it's sometimes covered with the snow.

I put lights on it each Christmas; it's as pretty as can be.
Lots of people stop to look at it, a beautiful sight to see!
My beautiful evergreen tree, on it I can depend;
no matter what the weather brings, it will not break or bend!

Sleep

My eyes are getting heavy, time to go to bed I say;
but I cannot really fall asleep, at the ending of the day.
I have so much I need to do, like homework for my class;
I must complete my assignment, if I expect to pass.
But I will take a nap now, and finish when I awake…
"Hi Mom, what time did you say it is?"
Oh, no, I think I'm late!

Sleep(less)

Night has come, but sleep has not arrived.
I wait in vain for it to overtake my mind.
No, I cannot embrace this wonderful feeling,
that envelopes my being and brings such healing.
Instead my body resists that tranquil thing called rest,
and stays awake, each hour to caress.
With folded hands and eye lids tightly closed,
I try to find that comfort and repose.

One sheep, two sheep, three sheep four,
yet sleep will not come knocking at my door.
Five sheep six sheep seven sheep eight,
please sleep come before it is too late;
I must get up and be dressed by eight,
but still on sleep, I continue to wait.
Nine sheep, ten sheep I count some more,
Finally, sleep comes knocking at my door!

Off to sleep my mind wanders in peaceful bliss;
this thing called sleep I can no more resist.
I rest and dream, and then I rest some more;
my mind takes flight to some far distant shore.
I lose control and let my body relish,
the moment I spend in unconscious bliss.
Then I awake refreshed and so revived;
ready to face the new day that's arrived.

I hope and pray that sleep will come my way,
when I'm tired and weary at the close of day!

Sunset Dreams

The fiery sunset sat upon a distant hill,
igniting all the dreams the night would bring;
and yet within her arms lay quietly,
the moment just before dark's stunning glee.
A time for just resting endlessly,
if sleep should come to eyes that long to see,
that blissful moment when all is truly still,
as we look out towards that distant hill.

Then, a soft voice whispers, "Peace be Still."
Be still and let your mind with sweet dreams fill,
and take you to the depths of various scenes,
where everything will feel oh so surreal.
Indulge yourself in all the glorious splendor,
as you dream on, in peaceful rest and slumber.
Awakened by the ringing of a bell,
that summons you to what, only time will tell.

We'll face the new day, yes as we arise,
with joyous thoughts of yesterday's reprise.
But as we hold on to our dreams untold,
we will proceed to walk upright and bold.
We'll face another day, still very new,
with strength to do just what we need to do.
We'll face all challenges that come our way,
cause we are blessed to see another day!

The Lonely One

She walks across the crowded room, "you look so good!", they said.
But they could not imagine, what was going on inside her head!
She felt so lonely and alone, although the crowd was great,
but all that she could think about, was how long she'd have to wait.

Can anybody see her, can someone feel her pain?
Can anybody tell, she feel like she's insane?
Oh no, they do not notice, as the music plays so loud;
everybody seems so happy, mingling among the crowd!
No one will stop and notice, in her eyes there is a stare;
no one will stop and notice, it's as if she isn't there.

The band will play its last song, *"Good night My Love"*, it is.
Lovers clinging to each other, as they dance, caress and kiss.
When the song was ended, no one made a move to leave;
after they played, *"The Party's Over"*, everyone split the scene.

The next day, they were all shocked, and they gazed in disbelief,
as they heard the news about Mary, it brought them so much grief.
Yes, after that grand party, Mary went home and cried,
she left a letter telling all, that she would rather die.

If only someone had noticed, the stare within her eyes.
If only someone had noticed, that she looked like she would cry.
This did not have to happen; she could be here today,
if only someone had taken the time and 'really' looked her way.

We are each other's keeper, that's what the Bible says;
if only someone had noticed, they could have said some prayers.
If only she had shared what was going on inside in her head,
if only someone had noticed, Mary Anne may not be dead!

Let's stroll some more...

The Makings of a Man

A man of courage, integrity and strength;
to live by these convictions, he'll go to great lengths.
These are the things that drive a man of faith,
to believe in his mission, and not hesitate!

Doing what he must, with the job at hand,
for he knows tomorrow is promised to no man.
He tries to make a difference in all he has to do,
so, that others can have a much better life, too.

It's not just about him and his family;
it's about all people and humanity.
People of all races, color and creed,
trying to practice the things they believe.

Liberty and justice aren't just words he recite,
they are human rights, for which he continually fights.
He stands for what he believes, and for less he won't fall,
until there is liberty and justice for "all"!

He's a people's man; and, believes in his heart,
that all men were made equal right from the start.
Inequality comes when some people begin,
to control the freedom God gave us, within.

Humility, service and self-sacrifice,
are the things that he's practiced, throughout his life.
He may not be perfect in every which way,
but he tries to live his best-life each and every day.

He keeps pressing, pushing, and doing what's right.
Conviction and honesty are his guiding lights.
When it's all said and done, here on this earth,
he'll move on to heaven, to continue his new birth.

There he'll go on living throughout eternity;
so, he lives life on earth, as God designed it to be!

The Winding Road

Don't think, think, think my sister that you can live the way you live,
and yet survive the streets.
Don't drink, drink, drink my brother to wash the pain away,
cause self-destruction brings defeat.

Some drugs to keep you sane, and a drink to ease the pain, is what you say;
but this can only lead to horror, and a life that seems so useless anyway.
You don't really want to go there, the road back is so long and cold,
and you may not like the people that you're sure to meet along the road!

Your body rocked in pain, as you cringe inside your tiny cell,
longing for some drugs or alcohol the pain to kill.
As your head is spinning and you feel you cannot cope,
you reach for any substance; be it opioid, alcohol, or dope.

And then, at last you come down from that high and feel so low,
as you search your mind and wonder, why there you chose to go.
Why did you choose to walk the long and winding road;
and not the one that leads to 'perfect' peace within your soul?

Think Men, Think

Think with the head God gave you, on your head,
not with the one that lies between your legs.
Don't let those foolish women convince you,
that you must do what they expect you to.

Men stand strong and steadfast, they don't fall
for everything that carries the name girl.
I'm not saying the temptation isn't real,
I'm not saying you won't want to cap a feel.

Men, think about the trouble this can start,
if you turn around and choose to break her heart.
A woman 'scorned' is not someone to mess with;
she will get back at you, you must believe it!

Think of the hurt you will cause your loved ones,
when everything is finally said and done.
You decide if it's really worth your time,
just to have another conquest on your line.

Where are your values oh dear man of honor?
Where is the pride that you should want to show her?
I guess it's hard for you to look her in the eyes,
and admit to telling all those lies.

If you have no interest, don't pursue it,
I promise that you'll just live to regret it.
Think men, think, just think about it,
and you may find, it really is not worth it!

Virtually Anything

The rapper's game is virtually anything,
it makes one wonder what rappers really sing.
Rapping this, and rapping that, not caring what…
Let's put a stop to that!

I'm coming at you with a style that's personal,
on second thought, it's virtually original.
Don't say you don't like, and then try to bite,
cause when I hit the mike it's going to be tight.

I'm laying this one down from the ground,
so, what you hear is my original sound.
Just let the rhythm move your feet;
the feeling you'll get is such a treat!

A Brooklyn-born native from the hood;
my motives sometimes misunderstood.
Just doing what's needed to survive,
and watching as some brothers take the dive.

Yes, virtually anything is the game we play,
and, that's the way we live from day to day.
Afraid to grasp reality, while trying to keep our sanity,
yet striving to reach our full ability.

So, rappers, strut your stuff, but keep it real;
let's teach the little ones just what's the deal.
Before we start to virtually exist, like in a mist,
let's know if we're being cheered or dis.

Be real, be true, don't be virtually you;
just know what you do, will stick like glue.
You don't have to do what others do, if it isn't you.
Be bold, be you, and to thine own self, be true!

Yes

I'm talented, yes. I'm blessed, yes.
I've tried to stand out from the rest, yes.
I've done what I've done; I've been all around,
I've taken and passed many tests, yes.

But, have I arrived, "no", there's much more inside,
I have not yet exhausted my mind.
For I truly know, that as onward I go,
I will never be one to say "No".

There's still much to learn, there's still much to change;
there will always be a chance to improve.
We must open our minds, and our spirits divine,
and say, yes, we are willing, there's room.

Oh, no, we can't stop, we must 'get to the top'.
there will always be things we can do!
So, my friend just live on, and when this day is gone,
tomorrow will soon welcome you.

As you open your eyes to a brand-new day,
just rejoice in your heart and be blessed!
Though you don't know the test, you can certainly rest
on the promises of God, and say, Yes!

Still more to reflect on...

Life Lessons and it's Seasons

And then it rained...

And then it rained, the water so refreshing.
And then it rained, the drops kept falling down.
And then it rained, the blue skies suddenly cloudy.
And then it rained; heavy raindrops hit the ground.

And then it rained, what happened to the sunshine?
Things all around now suddenly soaking wet!
What used to be a bright and sunny outlook,
now seemed to be too hopeless to forget!

And then, at last, a little ray of sunshine!
And then at last a reason to believe;
the dark clouds would soon start disappearing;
and sunshine skies would soon the clouds relieve.

And then at last, that little ray of sunshine,
turned into skies so blue and clouds so white!
No trace of rain, no dark clouds hovering over,
a sudden feeling, things will be alright!

And then at last, those skies once dark and dreary,
bursting with drenching rain from every seam;
now seemed so blue, with white clouds drifting slowly;
it almost seems like it was just a dream.

So, when life's challenges bring us gloom and darkness,
and rainy days that seem to never end;
just look up and catch that glimpse of sunshine,
and know bright days are just around the bend!

For, surely, as the day is dark and dreary,
with signs of relief to be seen nowhere,
keep looking up, don't doubt it for a moment;
and blue skies will once again appear!

In every rain cloud and with every raindrop falling,
remember there are lessons to be learned.
You may emerge a little wet and weary,
but what great knowledge and wisdom you'd have earned!!

As Time Goes By

Tick, Toc, Tick, Toc time marches on you know,
and yes, before you know it, your age will start to show.
Don't get me wrong, it doesn't matter, we'll all get there some day,
if we are blessed to live that long; if we do not pass away.
What bothers me, is all the time, we waste from day to day;
oh no, not time spent sleeping or relaxing in any way;
its time spent doing frivolous things like gossiping or fussing;
it's time spent meddling, drinking strong drinks and cussing;
it's time we choose to spend just backstabbing and backbiting;
it's the time we choose to spend just quarreling and fighting.

Dear friend, if we would take that time and put it to good use;
yes, use it to do something good, whatever we may choose.
Just think about the good things we could accomplish day by day.
Just think about the people we could help along the way.
Just think about the kind words we could speak to our neighbors.
Just think about the good deeds we could do with all those hours.
There are so many, many needs just waiting to be met,
so many children hungry, dying, how dare we forget?
Yes, every little second, every minute, every hour,
is time that we can use to do whatever is in our power!

There's work enough for everyone, no one needs to feel slighted,
in fact, the ones who work non-stop, for a rest would be delighted!
Rise up, go forth, march on with time; make your existence known;
then one day, you'll look back, and see just how much you have grown!
You'll grow in all the right ways; you'll gain respect for life.
You'll realize there's still hope, in all the pain and strife.
You'll gain a new perspective. You'll look life in the face.
You'll then be able to realize, that life is just a race.
And yes, as time goes by dear friend, and as you near life's end;
you will look back, and you will say, that it was time well spent!

64

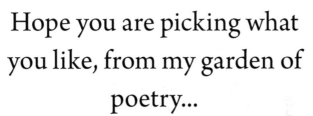

Hope you are picking what
you like, from my garden of
poetry...

As you enter Manhood…

You are now about to enter, a new phase of your life;
it is the phase called **"Manhood"**; what does that signify?
You may not feel that much has changed over the past years,
but, let's look back a little bit; it's not as it appears.

A baby born into the world solely depending on mom and dad;
you couldn't walk, you couldn't talk, but you were a joy to have.
The years went by; you learned new things, and mastered them by far;
beyond all expectations, you've shone quite like a star!

You learned to run, you learned to jump, you learned to do it all;
you learned to get up and move on, when you would sometimes fall.
You learned to love all people, and all things that God has made;
you learned your lessons well, as you went from grade to grade.

So, as you step in to **"Manhood"**, please make sure you understand,
the things you've learned will not change, because you're now a man.
What changes now is how you handle, the times of stress and strife.
What changes now is how you deal, with the challenges in your life.

When you become a man, you put away childish things;
not meaning that there won't be times to laugh and joke and sing.
It means that you will stand up for what's right, and do not fear.
It means that you will seek God, because He's always near.

Seek Him for He has for you, a life's purpose; and a plan.
Seek Him in all your hopes and dreams; He'll help you understand.
How do I seek Him you may ask, and that is only fair?
Seek Him through prayer and read His Word, He'll make it very clear!

In life there are no guarantees, but here's one I'll make to you;
if you follow God's instructions, He'll be there to see you through!
For every battle you must fight, for every test you face,
He will be there to fight for you, if you put Him in first place!

So, young man as you're about to enter into **"Manhood"**,
I hope that these instructions will be clearly understood.
God do love you, young man, He wants the best for you.
My prayer is that He'll bless you, in everything you do!

Baby Boy

A baby boy, oh how much joy
he'll bring to you, you'll see.
As he grows up, he'll make you laugh,
it will happen naturally.

Yes, boys are very special,
they do the strangest things.
Yet in between the mischief,
a lot of joy they bring.

So, enjoy your little baby boy,
cause he'll grow up so fast.
Yes, take the time to show him love,
a love you know will last.

Baby Girl

Enjoy your little baby girl,
the cutest in the world!
She'll grow up to be a big girl,
with lace and crimps and curls.

She will bring you so much joy,
as she plays with her favorite toys.
Her pretty eyes, her charming smile,
will soon have you hypnotized.

Baby girls are very special…
Sugar, spice, and all that's nice!
Yes, before you even know it,
you will be hooked for life!

Changes

Changes happen every day,
the sun comes up then it goes away,
the moon comes out, but it does not stay,
changes happen every day!

We get so comfortable in our own little world,
so when changes come, we are so appalled!
This cannot change, is what we say;
I have always known it to be this way!

But have you ever stopped and thought,
of the wonderful things change have brought?
Let's just imagine for a while,
where we would be without the changing tide!

There'll be no buses; there'll be no trains.
There'll be no cars; there'll be no planes.
There'll be no one for us to call,
cause, there'll be no telephone on the wall.
There'll be no lights for us to see;
oh, what a dark world this would be!

We all can name so many things,
that are all a part of what change brings.
We need just imagine for a minute,
what this world would be without change in it.

So, welcome change with open arms,
don't let it bring about alarm!
But, as we change, let's not forget,
that God, our Father, has not changed yet!

Let's strive for changes that honor life,
and not for ones that will cause strife.
Let's change to improve the human race,
let's change for better, by God's grace!

Changing Seasons

The leaves are changing colors, and falling from the trees.
The air has gotten chilly from the sudden autumn breeze.
It's time to put away our grills and all our summer thrills,
as we look forward to autumn, and the changes that it brings.

I can't believe how summer came and left us oh so soon!
Now for the autumn weather, we must all make some room.
Yes, summer was a lot of fun, with so many things to do;
at barbecues and swimming pools; we made new friends too!

But now, we must say, "so long", as she swishes swiftly by;
we feel so sad to see her go, we almost want to cry.
But don't you cry, enjoy this season, and please do not despair,
because, before you know it, she will return next year!

Changing Tides

There is that calm before the storm, we hear so much about;
there's so much peace, our spirits seize the chance to sing and shout!
But soon the sudden rolling of thunder can be heard;
the constant flash of lightening makes us scared to speak a word!
The skies grow dark, the rain begins and we suddenly realize,
that a thunder storm is brewing, right before our eyes.
Then before we know it, the skies begin to clear;
the thunders have subsided, and the rain's no longer there.
The sun will soon shine brightly; and clear up the dark sky.
Again, we've made it through the storm, although we thought we'd die!

College Bound

As you go off to college, let me give you some advice,
but first of all, I'd like to say, you have made a great choice!
High School is now behind you, and college is ahead;
much success now awaits you, there is nothing you should dread.

So, just go on, and do it; just do the best you can,
we will be here to help you, if you should need a hand.
Some days will be much harder, than others, that's for sure,
but the hard work will help you, your future to secure!

There's such a great future waiting for you to explore,
so be ready when opportunity, comes knocking at your door.
Be a leader, trail blazer, make paths others will follow.
Be open to ideas, don't be stubborn or too shallow.

You have already had, much success in your past;
keep doing what you're doing, and that success will last!
Then at the end of the day, when it's all said and done,
you'll receive your degree, and you'll know that you have won!!

Happy Birthday

Today is your birthday,
and oh, what a better way,
to celebrate your special day,
than to send wishes your way!

A wish first for God's blessings,
as you celebrate today,
and then a wish for lots of joy,
as you go along your way!

A wish for family and friends,
to help you share your day.
A wish that lots of special gifts,
will be sent your way today!

And as the day draws to a close,
and you sit down and reflect;
may there not be anything,
that you did, somehow, neglect.

And as you thank God for the day,
and the blessings He sent your way;
may He bless you with more birthdays,
like the one you had today!

Let's Celebrate

Christmas is the time of year when friends and family meet,
and joyous music fill the air with Christmas carols sweet.
A feeling of togetherness is felt by folks we greet;
with joy and laughter everywhere, and lots of Christmas treats.

But as we celebrate this year, let's focus on the reason,
for this great time of year, we call, the joyous Christmas season!
Let's celebrate the birth of hope and peace to all mankind.
Let's celebrate the hate and fear that we can leave behind!

Yes, as we sing, *Joy to the World*, let's sing with all our hearts;
let's sing until all hate and fear, we may have felt, depart!
For Christ is born, and now He reigns as king of all the earth;
what greater way to honor Him than to celebrate His birth!!

Let's move on...

January

Fierce winds are howling in the trees,
we really feel the winter breeze.
The trees are bare, there are no leaves,
except for on the evergreens.

Children playing in the snow,
making snowballs they can throw.
They also made a big snowman,
and dance around him hand in hand.

Yes, it is very cold outside,
so, under mittens their hands hide.
As they play, laugh, jump and run,
they do not seem to miss the sun.

So, old man winter strut your stuff,
for soon the spring will call your bluff.
Reign on; reign on, for a little while,
but when it's time, leave with a smile.

February

The days are long; the wind is strong,
the snow is falling on the ground!
The groundhog sights his shadow,
and proceeds to turn around and go.
Just six more weeks is what we hear,
before old man winter disappears.

Yes, soon we'll see the melting snow,
and we will sense our anxieties grow
We'll soon be able to glimpse a sign,
that old man winter has resigned.
Yes, once again the snow will melt,
we'll soon forget how winter felt.

March

Comes in like a lion, goes out like a lamb,
the saying is sometimes true,
because as winter leaves the stage,
there comes a calm that's new.

For this great month will usher in,
the end of winter's strife,
the time of year when earth will ring,
with feelings of new life.

As the season change and our clock we turn,
we'll see life springing from the grown.
The snow will melt with a little frown,
as springtime finally comes around.

April

April showers bring May flowers,
a rhyme that's oh so true.
With each small raindrop that falls,
the flowers will bloom a new.

Yes, April is a pretty month,
right in the middle of spring,
It's when we celebrate Easter,
and the Easter bunny thing.

It is a very special month,
of hope and joy and peace,
as we put winter behind us,
and watch our joys increase.

April, I love April, it sounds so very girlish,
It is month that I am sure, I will always cherish!

May

The rain has fallen from the sky,
but now the ground is pretty dry.
The flowers are now in full bloom,
and the butterflies will enter soon.

The air is fresh, the grass is green.
summer will soon be on the scene.
But until then, we'll be glad and sing,
of the wonderful magic May skies bring.

June

The flowers are all in full bloom,
it's the beautiful month of June!
Spring is almost at an end,
and summer's just around the bend.

School is almost done,
time for lots of fun!
Happy children all around,
running and playing in the sun.

They'll look forward to summer time.
They'll leave the books and studies behind.
They'll relax and frolic in the sun,
because they know all their school work's done!

July

Bang, bang the fireworks take to the sky,
amidst the crowds and distance, they fly.
As we rejoice and celebrate,
the independence of a land so great!

We wear our red, white and blue,
and to our flag, honor is due.
Yes, as great July slips away,
we'll long remember that special day!

August

Along comes August, hot and dry,
there's no rain falling from the sky.
The grass is longing for some rain,
but the summer skies, it cannot drain.

Happy families far and near,
enjoy love ones that they hold dear.
The privilege to work and play,
is enjoyed by all from day to day.

September

The time of year has come and so,
it's back to school the children go!
They'll meet new friends and chat with old,
and many stories will be told.

Yes, summer days they held such fun,
but now the schoolwork has begun.
They'll work real hard throughout the term,
but for the summer days they'll yearn.

October

Ghost and goblins are the theme of the day,
as children rush to ride in the hay.
There'll be trick-o-treating all around,
as they listen in silence to the scary sounds.
There'll be things that go bump in the night,
and all the children will scream with fright!

Children going from door to door,
never really knowing what's in store.
Adults dressed in weird costumes,
so no one will know them as they enter the room.
Yes, October is a scary month,
when the ghosts and goblins all come out!

November

November skies are turning gray,
snow must certainly be on the way.
Families gather from far and near,
to give God thanks for another year.
There are lots of laughter, to be found,
as friends and family gather all around.

The turkey is king for a day,
as families close their eyes to pray.
They thank God for His many blessings,
as they view the turkey filled with dressing.
And when it's finally time to go,
they must go out and face the snow.

December

Yes, snow has finally hit the ground,
and all the children gather round.
With happy faces smiling bright,
they sing and frolic with delight.

Yes, it's their favorite time of year,
for they know Santa will soon be here!
Faces stare with joy and glee,
at presents under the Christmas tree!

But, most of all we sing the song,
that Jesus, the Christ child is born.
And as the year's last shadows dim,
may peace and joy ring the New Year in!

RESPECT

R - is for **remembering** how to treat each other.

E - every **effort** should be made or else why even bother.

S - a **simple** thoughtful act could go a long, long way,

P - to **prove** your love for each other day by day.

E - yes **even** when it's hard to admit that you are sorry,

C - just **count** the cost, and you will do it in a hurry.

T - **thoughtfulness** that's how it has to be,
　　I have respect for you, and you have respect for me!

Signs of Summer

The trees are blowing in the wind, as the butterflies float by.
The birds are singing in the trees, and flying high in the sky.
Yes, nature has now come alive; awaken from its sleep,
and now it's time to have some fun, after winter's long retreat!

Yes, soon it will be summer, we can feel it everywhere;
soon spring will make its exit, until sometime next year.
There'll be lots of time for laughing and play in the sun;
we'll have a lot of good time, before the summer's done!

Some

Some we pass by the wayside and just whisper "Hi".
Some come into our lives and stay there for a while.
For every chance meeting, there's a purpose; a plan;
it's never a coincidence, that we must understand.

Some enter into our lives and just seem to bring stress;
by the time that they are gone, our life seems a mess!
But if we look closely, we may have to confess,
and say to ourselves, "yes", that was just a "test".

Some come and then go, in and out our lives,
teaching us lessons to help make us wise.
If we'd only take heed of the lessons and learn,
wisdom, knowledge and understanding we'll earn.

Some lessons we learn are joyous and thrilling!
Some lessons we learn are oh, so fulfilling!
Then there are those lessons that's not very good;
there're also, those lessons that's misunderstood.

So, under some pressure and under some stress,
just continue to focus on being your best.
There will be a time when you will overcome,
yes, success will be your, when all's said and done!

Spring Forth

Spring! What does it mean...
new thoughts, new hopes, new dreams!
A time for reflection, a time for change,
as we awake from a winter of rage.

We open our eyes to a whole new life,
springing forth from a winter of strife.
Spring gives us hope to know all's not lost,
in the snow, and in the cold winter frost!

It's a time for rejoicing and for planning
vacations and travel and such,
as we visit with family, friends and others,
with whom we have been out of touch.

Spring is exciting, and don't you just love,
the feeling of new life it brings?
So, let's all rejoice in this season of new birth,
God created in His scheme of things!

The Graduate

Today, as you graduate, you make us very proud;
we'd like to stand on a mountaintop and shout it out real loud!
So, all the world would truly know how proud we are of you,
but, in the meantime, in-between time, this wish will have to do.

But on a much more serious note, we would like for you to know,
you have achieved such great success, just had to tell you so.
For all the times you thought about just giving up the fight,
we know today you are very glad; you chose to do what's right.

You should be proud of this great task God helped you to complete.
You stood your ground, finished your course you would not take defeat!
And, so today, we all rejoice in all you have achieved,
it really shows that we can do what ere our minds perceive.

You've learned so many great things. but there are lots more to learn.
As you go on to grad school, your Master's you will earn.
But promise you will never forget, as down life's part you go,
the most important things in life, come from the heart, you know!

So, walk dear one in God's light, let Him direct your part,
let Him walk before you, let Him live within your heart.
And if you only do this, you will have great success;
in all you do, in all you say, you'll stand out from the rest!

The Test

You've finished the subject matter; you've given it your best,
but before the course is ended, you must first pass the test!
For, how else can you prove, just how much you have learned;
how else will people know if your credits you have earned?
Yes, friend the "test", it is a "must", if you will claim success;
before you start to practice, you must first pass the test!

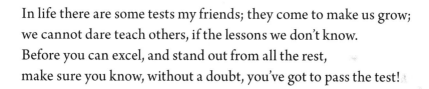

They place the test before you, some you complete with ease;
some of it is so easy; you say, "it is a breeze!"
Then, finally you stumble on a problem so 'severe',
you search for the right answer, but find it is not there.
You'll come back to it you say, on completing all the rest,
cause, before the course is ended, you 'must' first pass the test!

In life there are some tests my friends; they come to make us grow;
we cannot dare teach others, if the lessons we don't know.
Before you can excel, and stand out from all the rest,
make sure you know, without a doubt, you've got to pass the test!

Time

The days turned into weeks; the weeks turned into months.
The months turned into years, where did time go, she says.
It seems like yesterday was just here, and now it's gone!
It seems like only yesterday; my little ones were born!

Time marches on, so don't you sleep, because before you know it,
you would have had something to do, and you didn't even do it!
No, don't be fooled by old man time, it's later than you think;
start doing what you're called to do, time's gone before you wink!

Yes, there're still many seas to cross, and many fences you can mend;
so, work while there is still time left, you'll be happier in the end.
For what greater joy can there be, than to know you used time well,
as we gather around God's heavenly throne, our earthly tales to tell?

Time is a gift, just treasure it, like you would any other;
don't think it will always be there, so you don't have to bother!
No, time rolls on and on and on it's continually on the move;
it will not wait for you or me; we must get with the groove.

Yes, old man time, misunderstood, by oh so many people;
we set him high up on a shelf, we put him on the steeple.
Then each day we watch the hands as they just tick away,
knowing that the end of time, will come for us one day!

Celebrating 100 Years

I must begin by saying, it is a blessing to have spent
a hundred years on this earth,; too much to comprehend!
You've seen so many changes, been through so many things.
I could only try to imagine the knowledge that it brings!

At the moment of conception, is where it all began,
a baby that grew up fast, and soon learned to take a stand.
Yes, God has really blessed you, look how the family's grown,
from children, to great-great-grand's, what a heritage you've sown!

And so, it's been 100 years, and you've lived to see it all;
there have been lots of blessings, too many to recall!
Yes, you can truly say, you're in a class all by yourself;
God chose to shine His love on you, for all those "100" years!

Your coming in; and your going out, He has watched over you;
He truly grants you "favor" in everything you do.
Yet, still, it is not over; live each day like it's your last,
and God will keep on blessing you, as He's done in the past!

Some serious moments...

Our Country and it's Politics

911

On 9/11 the call went out, emergency in the sky,
America had been attacked, and lots of folks would die!
We did not see it coming, when it happened, some folks said!
We did not have the answers, as we buried our dead.

We woke up to a new day, business as usual we thought,
not knowing that before days end, a refuge would be sought.
Not knowing the twin towers would both come tumbling down,
and that a hijacked plane, would hit the Pentagon;
as yet another hijacked plane would come crashing to the ground.

So many senseless lives were lost in this great tragedy.
How would we ever get pass this? We need a remedy!
We need to understand and know that God was not asleep;
there is a hidden reason for this tragedy so deep!

Could God want our attention?
Did we lose His protection?
Could He be saying to us that He wants our full attention,
because we have strayed way too far in our own direction?

I don't think so, we ponder and try desperately to conclude,
God would not put his people through this painful solitude.
Oh, we all know the consequences a life of sin will bring,
yet, time and time again, we tend to let old Satan in.

The only way that we can truly find God's grace,
is to fall down on our knees and pray and seek His face.
Then, and only then, with loving outstretched hands,
will He in grace and mercy intervene and save our land.

We cannot do it on our own,
we need to kneel before God's throne.
We need to ask God to forgive,
the sinful way that we have lived.

911, emergency! Going straight up to the sky;
we are calling on you great God, before more people die!
Dispatch your angels throughout the land,
and stop the terror from our enemy's hand!

How wonderful it is to know that we can call on You,
So, **911** we're calling; we hope our call gets through!

Barack Obama's Victory Poems

And so...

And so, we waited, waited with excitement and delight,
to find out who would be our president that night!
Then, finally at 11 p.m. on the hour,
word came, the winner was Barack Obama!
The crowds exploded with mixed emotions everywhere,
laughing, shouting, crying, jumping in the air!
All colors, black, white, yellow, red, and brown,
not caring as they danced and jumped around.
It was a scene the world will never forget,
It brought us all together with no regrets.
Oh no, not just Americans were overjoyed,
excitement stretched from Africa, to Hanoi!
So many people celebrating this victory!
What a great event for the world to see!
All Americans coming together as one!
And yes, the time for change has now begun!
Yes, "Change" is what Barack Obama campaigned on,
and, clearly, it's the reason why he won!!

Mesmerized...

Like a new day dawning, and the people waiting to see the light,
they stood hypnotized, like a deer staring at the car's bright light.
Waiting to hear who would be the next president,
and would there be any voter incidents.
"I have a dream", Martin Luther King once said,
"that one day people would be judged by the contents
of their character, and not be the color of their skin."
Forty years in coming was this dream of Martin Luther King!
A lot of us stopped dreaming and was feeling oh so sad,
not knowing that a child was born, and his journey had begun.

Barack Obama, born to an African father and white mother;
raised, mainly, by his white grandmother and grandfather.
Not by chance, but by God's plan oh so divine,
knowing he would be the one to bridge the racial divide.
His childhood journeys took him to several distant lands,
like Hawaii and Indonesia where he learned to understand.
He understood that people may be different everywhere,
but he also understood that there are many things we share.
Then finally this young man had the **audacity to hope,**
that one day he could be president, when others said he won't.
And so he chose to run for the greatest office in the land,
and yes, the rest is history, Obama is our Man!!

A Phenomenon...

A phenomenon has taken place; mere words cannot express,
the feeling of excitement, we as a race possess!
But yet, it transcends beyond race, more than we can perceive;
it's **faith** and **hope** and **love** and **dreams**, things in which we believe.
A **faith** that has guided us, when the evidence we did not see!
A **hope** that has sustained us, beyond reality!
A **love** for our dear country, though many faults we see,
A **dream** we kept on dreaming, though it seemed an impossibility!
These things have brought us to this day of joy and jubilation.
These things must move us forward, through many tribulations.
We must not stop, though we can rest, for there's much work to be done,
before this country can proclaim, the victory's been won!

Brave Soldiers

The time has come for fighting,
brave soldiers march to war!
With made-up-minds and painful hearts,
they travel distance far!
They know they're on a mission,
the job they must complete!
They will not cringe or tremble;
they will not take defeat!
So, on they march through unknown lands,
not knowing what's ahead,
just knowing that the enemy,
would love to see them dead!
Yes, in the face of terror,
our brave soldiers still march on;
they hunger to taste victory,
and hope it won't be long!

Crisis

So, you think **ISIS** bad…meet a cop on your journey;
he's trying to take your life in a hurry!
Oh no, not in Afghanistan, Syria or Iran,
I'm talking about our great **USA**, man!

Ain't safe nowhere if your skin is black;
almost feel like slavery is on its way back!
But we must stand strong, put our trust in God;
continue to pray, though He already heard!

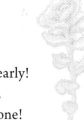

Don't pray to Mohamed, Buddha or Mary,
the only one who can save us, is the son she loved dearly!
Stand strong, have faith, God's still looking on,
and before we know it, **BOOM**, the wicked ones gone!

He promised He'll fight our battles and win;
we have nothing to lose, and everything to gain.
Don't give up the fight, just continue to strive,
for justice and equality, as we, "keep hope alive"!

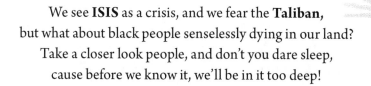

We see **ISIS** as a crisis, and we fear the **Taliban,**
but what about black people senselessly dying in our land?
Take a closer look people, and don't you dare sleep,
cause before we know it, we'll be in it too deep!

Let's clean up this mess, turn our hearts to the **Man,**
The one who can save us, and heal our great land!
His name is **Jesus**, in case you don't know;
if you have any questions, the **Bible** says so!

Hurricane Katrina

Like a thief in the night you came, but not so quietly;
destroying what has always been a great society.
Ravaging thorough the city, stealing lives and homes and land,
with no regard for anything that, in your way would stand!
Breaking trees, leveling houses, with so much rage and wrath,
as you traveled, swiftly, down your self-destructive part!
Not caring who might be the victims in your way,
or that they might not live to see another day.

Ravaging towns, and highways, making all seem small,
as viewed from heights we saw the horror of it all!
Destroying lives and families, destroying hopes and dreams,
destruction that would never end, at least that's how it seemed.
Destroying all those things that we held dear in our lives,
but yet, unable to destroy that strong will to survive!
That "will" to rise again from such a devastating blow;
that "will" to carry on when everything within say's no!

And so, we build back houses, bridges, stores and dams!
And so, we build back schools, hospitals on that leveled land.
Making plans to build levees that will hold the water back,
should other storms stand lurking, in the future to attack.

And as we build, we build our strength and character for sure.
And as we build, we build our hopes and dreams once more.
And as we build, we build our faith in God, and feel secure.
His hand was in our hands, and of that we're very sure!

But why did He let us endure such devastating pain?
We ask this single question o'er and o'er again!
If we are honest with ourselves, we will truly see,
lots of the blame for what took place, lies with you and me.
God did not build those levees, no, they were made by man;

why blame Him if the raging storm, they could not withstand?
Yes, there is something that we need to really understand;
we have chosen to neglect God, and lots of His commands!

But God has promised us, that He would 'still' heal the land,
if we would humble ourselves, call on Him, and take a stand.
Somehow, I feel that He is just vying for our attention;
we need to heed before there are, more serious devastations!

I Can't Breathe

I can't breathe, I can't breathe, that's what George Floyd cried,
as he laid there on the pavement, where he finally died.
A modern-day lynching is what comes to my mind,
praying his dying will save mankind from more vicious, crimes!
The crimes are called, 'racism', 'injustice' and 'defeat'; They're
called 'police brutality', like we see on the streets.
I dare to make a parallel with my dear Savior's death,
as He stood there on the cross and He took His last breath.
George Floyd, however, was forced to the ground;
his life was taken from him, as all stood around.
With a foot to his neck, he paid the ultimate price;
though not there to witness, it didn't escape our eyes!

Then we wonder why people are so enraged;
not only black people, but people of every race.
Why in so many countries this death resonates?
God's bringing attention to injustice and hate!
So, let's not continue in an environment of hate;
let's try to correct it, before it's too late!
Because, when one hurts, we all feel the pain,
and it will continually haunt us, again and again.
Yes, It will eventually, somehow, "trickle" down,
cause, we know, what goes around, come around!
When we create an environment of hate,
how do we think we will somehow escape?

Let's make a change, "Americans", let's turn the raging tides;
let's bring peace to our nation, while freedom still abides. Let's
make laws that protects us 'all' from prejudice and hate; let's
select leaders that will serve 'all' people states!
Let's go back to the Bible, where Jesus said how,
there's faith, hope and love...but the greatest is Love!
Let's practice these teachings from the Bible, we must;

and live by our motto; that, "In God we trust"!
There's no other way that our country can be:
The land of the brave, and the home of the free!
Yes, if we would let justice and equality reign,
what happened to George Floyd, should 'never' happen again!

In God We Trust

A new year now unfolds,
with stories yet untold;
in search of peace and honor,
our soldiers face such horror!
Our country is engaged in war,
one like we have not seen this far.
Brave soldiers put their lives at stake,
and for a sign of peace we wait.
But as we wait, don't hesitate,
let's send up prayers to Heaven's gate.
We need that guidance from above.
We need to feel the Savior's love.
Don't get disgruntled and upset,
our Father has not failed us yet!
Think of the price our fore-fathers paid,
for us to have the life we've made.
Think on the past, indeed we must,
and never forget, "In God We Trust"!

Lessons Learned from 911

The years have passed, so very fast,
we wonder how long the pain would last.
I'll dare to say it will never end,
so we go on living and trying to make amends.

But, what did we learn from this tragedy,
that shook our country so severely?
It touched the core of our great land,
and now we look back, still united we stand!

Yes, great unity was seen that day,
as people bonded together in total dismay.
We all saw how very fragile life could be,
so, don't take it for granted is my greatest plea!

Show love each day, to the ones you hold dear,
let them always know just how much you care.
In doing so, all the world then will see,
what lessons we learned from this great tragedy.

Remembering the Dreamer and the Dream

Dr. Martin Luther King, a great man of God,
stood for freedom, equality and justice for all!
He fought courageously, never retreating,
for the 'inalienable' rights we were all given by God!
A man of knowledge, wisdom, understanding,
a man who listened to the Master's call!
His many sermons and speeches, as we will recall,
echoed…freedom, equality, justice for all!

Dr. Martin Luther King, a man of peace,
yet called to face the tides of turmoil and unrest.
This peaceful man, strong in his convictions,
knew that he must somehow past the test.
And so, with **'peaceful'** demonstrations,
he fought for rights he knew we must attain.
He knew that violence would only stir up violence,
and in the end, there won't be much gain.

Dr. Martin Luther King, he kept the faith;
he said that he had seen the Promised Land!
He said he may 'not' get there with us,
but he had a glimpse of '**just**' what was at-hand!
Yes, in his mountaintop experience,
he knew that God would bring his dream to pass,
he kept on trusting and believing,
that as a people, we would be free at last!

And though the dreamer died, his dream lives on,
and today we are seeing it come to past.
We see so many changes that he spoke of,
finally coming through for us at last!
But brothers, sisters don't get too complacent,
no, we have not yet, "finally" arrived!

We must keep moving forward like brave soldiers,
until all his dreams are realized!
We must keep preaching, teaching, the next generation,
so, they too will keep the dream alive.
Too many people lost their lives to gain the freedoms,
that we today are privileged to enjoy!
So, let's keep praying and seeking God's direction,
no matter how hopeless things may seem.
Let's 'ever' hold on to God's promises,
while remembering the **dreamer** and the **dream!**

The Protest

They walk the streets with posters, protesting what's unfair.
There are loud cries for justice, but no one seems to hear.
And with each cry comes outbursts, yes, it is very clear,
that justice must somehow prevail, no other course seems fair.

If we will finally conquer and a victory be won;
we must all get together and do what must be done.
Yes, then, and only then can we march on as one,
singing that old familiar song, *We Shall Overcome.*

Our protest is for freedom to live life as we please.
Our protest is for justice, all injustices to ease.
Our protest is in hopes that the fighting will soon cease.
Our protest is in faith that one day we'll be at peace.

So, we walk the streets protesting, in a very peaceful way.
Our signs and posters tell it all, so there's not much to say.
Yes, in great numbers there is strength, to face another day;
we will not stop until we're heard, we will not be sent away!

So much to think about...

The System

"Well, that's the way 'The System" works", been said too many times;
as a long, trail of mishaps and failures, is riding on that line.
Whose fault is it? Me, not me! You, oh hell, no!
We just know that's the way it works, they all will tell you so.

So, has the repairman been called?
Cause 'The System" is due for an overhaul!
"What's wrong with it?" This is the question many ask;
the answer to this question, still remains a task.

"Why haven't we seen 'The System" work for all?"
This burning question echoes from wall to wall.
"It takes time to fix, the things we need to fix."
Yes, that we understand, but there are too many other tricks!

Let's overhaul 'The System", let's bring it to its knees;
'The System" breathes injustice, with which we are not pleased.
We have suffered as a people, long enough I do believe,
I think it's time to focus on what we know we must receive.

We must receive some justice; it's been coming way to long.
We must stand up and fight for what we know is very wrong.
We have paid the price we've fought wars in countries everywhere;
now it's time for us to stand and fight for what we need right here!

Fix 'The System" of injustice and police brutality.
Fix 'The System" of racism which we experience constantly.
Fix 'The System" of lower income, because of the color of your skin,
Fix 'The System" of education, give equal opportunities within.

We're not asking for 'special' treatment, that is not what we believe.
We're asking for 'equal' treatment, like others now receive.
We want an even playing field, in all we do and say,
not one rule works for one race, but the other you turn way.

Overhaul the Justice System, do what must be done!
Break down unfair practices, only then would we have won!
Won the great Emancipation Proclamation's call;
as the land of, 'life, 'liberty' and 'justice' for all!

The land of the free, and the home of the brave,
we here it being uttered, time and time again.
So, let's fix The System, it's been 'too' long delayed,
the price has been paid, 'over' and 'over' again!

We Paused

The horror of it all, cannot be penned in words,
a day that we will not forget, made everybody pause.
We paused to remember, loved ones and family lost,
we thought about the future and how much it would cost.
Yes, we all stopped and pondered at the horror in the sky;
it left us all in shock and pain as we paused to wonder, why?
Why would people be so cruel, with no regard for life?
Why would they use innocent people in the center of their strife?
Why, oh why that is the cry that's heard from near and far,
as we try to make some sense of something that is so bizarre!

So we move on in hope...

Where Is Justice?

You asked for him, let's see if we can find him.
Riding in the van with three young men,
on the way to a basketball event.
Oops, he wasn't there, the punishment was not severe.

Someone shouted, "Check out Mr. Amadou Diallo".
'Justice' may have gone to see what's up with that.
Four cops, 41 shots, if he stopped by, no one saw him,
and then again, perhaps they just ignored him.

A woman threw away her newborn baby and kept on dancing,
damn, where was 'Justice', was he somewhere sleeping?
Was he not present when she received her sentence?
Now she walks the street with no repentance!

George Zimmerman, you say, did he see 'Justice'?
They probably met, then went their separate ways.
Cause if by chance they'd had a close encounter,
he probably wouldn't be walking the streets these days.

We must find 'Justice', he's important to our survival,
if not, then we must not bring men to trial.
Who is 'Trial'? How dare him stand alone?
'Trial' and 'Justice' must stand together and be known!

Many a young black men in search of 'Justice',
have heard about him, but they just can't trust this.
His name is mentioned as their 'trial' proceeds,
but once it's over, he is never on the scene.

Come let's find 'Justice'...tell 'Justice' not to run;
we need him for the next poor mother's son.
Before some hurting mother stands there weeping,
cause 'Justice' was not present, but somewhere sleeping.

Let's find 'Justice', we need him in our courtrooms,
we talk about him as we pledge our flag and sing our tunes.
We talk about him, oh, but he is missing,
so, in reality, we may as well dismiss him!

'Justice', it's been a long time since we've seen you;
too many 'injustices' we have been through!
If you don't show up soon and take your rightful place, then,
your impostor, 'Injustice', we will constantly embrace!

Things will get better;
let's walk by faith...

Religion as a Relationship

Almost Don't Count

Almost crusaded, but the Pastor said, "don't go."
Almost persuaded, Pontius Pilate told Paul so.
Almost dissuaded, by his friends, but he said, "no".

Almost don't count.

Almost done, but the cake fell anyhow.
Almost won, but we lost the game somehow.
Almost fun, but the teacher said stop now.

Almost don't count.

Almost petty, but the cash flow was too heavy.
Almost steady, but the couple were not ready.
Almost Freddie but his Mom said, "call him Teddy."

Almost don't count.

Almost crusaded, almost persuade, almost dissuaded.
Almost don't count.

Almost done, almost won, almost fun.
Almost don't count.

Almost petty, almost steady, almost Freddie.
Almost don't count.

We've all had situations, where "almost" was an issue.
There have been times that someone came running to our rescue,
because we almost tripped; we almost fell; we almost flipped.
They wasted time, and energy, I will be very blunt,
cause, 'almost' don't count!

Anchored

Out on the water the boats stand, as I sit here on the shore;
as they toss, and rock, and sway; I wonder if they are secure?
They move a little distance, not too far from where they stand,
because they have been anchored somewhere beneath the sand.

That anchor is the central point that keeps them stabilized;
it is what keeps them grounded, this I soon realize!
Then as that thought came to me, it suddenly became so clear;
"if we are anchored in Jesus, there is 'nothing' we should fear!"

Yes, like the boats on the waters, we will be tossed about;
sometimes we'll feel like the waves of life will truly knock us out!
But, as long as we are grounded in God's Word and in prayer,
we will be able to withstand it all, we can truly persevere!

So, don't go out on the waters, in the boat of life alone;
take 'Jesus' as your anchor, for your sins He has atoned.
And when the waves start raging, and the fear you cannot hide,
just know you're safely anchored, with 'Jesus' by your side!

Don't Mourn Me

Don't mourn for me, I'll be in glory, with my Savior, Lord and Friend!
Don't mourn for me, it is not the end, I've have just begun to live again!
The songs and poems that is written, describing how Heaven is,
pales in the reality of the real things, no man can describe this!
Yes, everything that's being sung, and written about you'll see,
but eyes cannot see and ears cannot hear, what is 'truly' the reality!
Folks, don't miss out on this great place, there's no other place like it;
so, whatever you have to do on earth, make sure that it is fixed!
Get ready for your trip to that place God's prepared for us;
but don't forget your ticket, for that 'ticket' is a 'must'!

God's Woman

(This is my signature poem)

I am God's woman, gentle kind and true.
I am God's woman, devoted Lord to you.
Like Ruth, I will not leave Thee, but follow You all my days,
I am Your woman, Lord; I will seek to know Your ways.

I am God's woman, as I toil along life's way.
I am God's woman as I live from day to day.
Like Esther, I'll be bold, and strong in every way,
I am Your woman Lord; I will live for You each day.

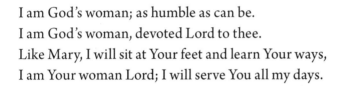

I am God's woman; as humble as can be.
I am God's woman, devoted Lord to thee.
Like Mary, I will sit at Your feet and learn Your ways,
I am Your woman Lord; I will serve You all my days.

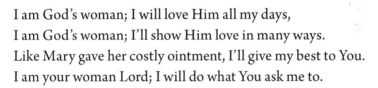

I am God's woman; I will love Him all my days,
I am God's woman; I'll show Him love in many ways.
Like Mary gave her costly ointment, I'll give my best to You.
I am your woman Lord; I will do what You ask me to.

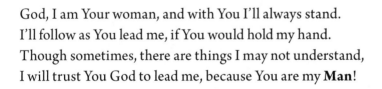

God, I am Your woman, and with You I'll always stand.
I'll follow as You lead me, if You would hold my hand.
Though sometimes, there are things I may not understand,
I will trust You God to lead me, because You are my **Man**!

Great Heights

My stature may not command what I am meant to be;
my true image you may not see, but there's a person inside of me.
I may not reach out very far, because of my size, you see;
don't be fooled by the outside, there's this person inside of me!

Yes, I can climb great mountains and reach up to the top,
and I can run for great lengths, without the need to stop!
No matter what the height or length, these feats I can attain,
as long as I have 'Christ' with me and in His strength remain!

There is no task too great for me, no job I can't accomplish;
He will give me whatever I need; my God, He is not selfish.
He wants the best for His children, like my parents, I recall;
but God can truly give the best, because He owns it all!

So set your goals, and set them high; forget how small you feel;
yes, He will truly give you, whatever help you need!
The "key" is living for Him, and giving Him control;
then He will pour out blessings, so many yet untold!

I Thank You

There's nothing else I can do, but to trust You.
There's nothing else I want to do, but to bless Your name.
So, today I say, "You've been with me all the way,
and I will trust You each and every day."

There's nothing I can do, but to praise You.
There's nothing I want to do but to thank You Lord.
You have been my friend, and will be till the end,
and for Your constant presence Lord, I thank You!

A friend whose always there, a friend whose always near.
What more can anyone ask of You?
I don't need nothing more; You're all I need for sure;
so, I'll thank You now and forevermore!

Lifetime Guarantee

The watch says, "Lifetime Guarantee";
the iron says it too.
It would be nice if this life held,
guarantees for me and you.

But, no, it doesn't work like that,
life holds no guarantees;
we must not live as if by 'chance',
can't live life as we please.

So, let's live the best life that we can;
take care of what God gave us.
Do right by others along the way,
as the Ten Commandments tell us!

Cause, then and only then, will we have
a "Heavenly" guarantee,
that we will reign with God one day,
throughout eternity!

Lord, it's all about You

Lord it's on You

Lord, I'll be what You want me to be,
I'll see as You want me to see…
This day Lord, it's on You!

Lord, I'll say what you want me to say,
I'll pray what you want me to pray…
This day Lord, it's on You!

Lord, I'll go where You want me to go,
and seeds of good works I will sow…
This day Lord, it's on You!

So, in obedience as you lead,
Your voice I will always heed.
I'll follow as You lead…
cause, it's on You!

Blessings

Thank you Lord for little blessings,
I love them every one.
Thank you God for all your goodness,
and all that you have done!

Thank you God for all your kindness,
and promises divine.
Thank you, Lord, for all your blessings,
You've been faithful every time!

Lord of all Creation

The Lord of all creation, so wondrous, kind and true,
make yourself known to us Lord, by everything you do.
Help us to depend on you, as you increase our faith.
Help us to not get weary, as on you, Dear Lord, we wait.

Rest

In this peaceful place, yes this restful place,
on you dear Lord I call.
Bring me rest, and peace, and comfort,
as on my knees I fall.
For there is not another, so faithful, kind and true,
so help me Lord, in all I do, to be more like you.

In My Quiet Time

In my quiet time, I listen for God's voice,
I hear Him whisper sweetly to my soul.
It's in my quiet time; I can hear a word from God,
a word that comforts me and make me whole!

In my quiet time is when I listen,
as He whispers ever sweetly in my ear.
His gentle voice I hear, nothing else compares,
as He lets me know that He is, oh, so near!

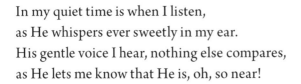

Speak to me Lord, speak to me gently;
open up my heart and ears to you.
Speak to me Lord, speak to me gently;
let me hear and do whatever you ask me to.

Love of a Father

God gave us earthly fathers, with wisdom to impart.
A father loves his children, with all that's in his heart.
He will not hurt His little ones; he keeps them from harm,
He protects them from all danger, as they walk arm in arm.

If our earthly fathers, can such love on us bestow,
think on the love we will receive, as God compassion shows.
Think on the many blessings, He has in store for us,
all He asks is that we love Him, and in Him always trust.

Our heavenly Father loves us; He's the greatest dad of all.
He promised He would save us, when on His name we call.
So if we'll only trust Him, and take Him at His word,
we will have no regrets, if we choose Him as our Lord!

Our Father

Our Father, who art in Heaven…the greatest dad of all!
Incline your ears to hear us, as we your children call.
You are our prime example, of what a dad should be;
help us to emulate You, so our children, your love will see.

Mother

A mother is a precious gift, sent from God above,
Lord, make us Godly mothers, as we show our children love.
Help us to teach them of You; help them to learn Your ways;
we want to be examples; they can follow all their days.

My Assignment

Our Savior paid the ultimate price, by dying on the cross!
Is there any price too high to pay, for loved ones that are lost?
I'll pay the price; I'll bear the pain that hurts so deep inside;
because I know what I must do, if Christ in me abides.

God spoke to me one morning, with instructions very clear.
I did not comprehend it all, so I did have some fears.
But God told me to be "fearless" and in Him only trust,
He said, "I will be with you, there is no need to fuss."

In the time I spent, "alone", with God, I truly watched Him move;
in things I least expected, in ways I did not choose.
He gave me revelations, and insights not once seen;
it's been my "greatest" pleasure, on my Dear God to lean!

And so, as I move forward, though I feel a little weak,
I have a sense within me, God's assignment I'll complete.
So, what will I do with all this, as I move on in Christ?
As I've already stated, someone must pay the price!

And so, with prayer and fasting, and much intersession too,
I'll bring my needs before my God, and He'll know what to do.
I'll lay them at His altar, believing in His Word,
and expecting him to answer, for, "after all" He's God!

He's the Alpha and Omega, the beginning and the end,
He's the God that we can trust in, and "always" can depend!
So, though the task seems daunting to little dear old me,
You are my God, in whom I trust, with this, "Special Delivery"!!

My Source

You are that electrifying power that lights up my life;
showing me, where to go, and what to do.
Yes, I know You will continue to lead me,
as long as I stay "plugged" in, Lord, to You.

You light my way, when days look dark and dreary.
You give me comfort that I'm not alone.
And when the night falls, and I'm feeling lonely,
You make me know that I'm Your very own.

You encourage me whenever I get weary.
You tell me just go on, I'll make you strong.
Some days when I feel like just quitting,
You give me strength to face another storm.

Lord, my prayer is that I stay "plugged" in to You,
that electrifying source that lights my life!
I won't overload and trip that circuit that connects us,
because I will be lost without Your light.

Lord, so, I'll do whatever You ask me to,
so, I can stay "connected" God, to You.
Walk with me, talk with me; keep me ever in Your presence;
You are my "source"; without You, there is "nothing" I can do!

Picture Perfect

My eyes behold the beauty of a picture-perfect world,
as I sit here on a bench, by the beach, and look on.
The seagulls singing, the breeze blowing, igniting my very soul;
how could I not be thankful, for the beauty I behold?

As I look out across the seas, with waters oh, so blue;
the sky, the clouds, the hills, the trees; they all come into view.
And in the far-off distance, where my eyes can see no more;
the sea and sky they seem to meet, as I sit here on the shore.

It's then I start to wonder, how can I help myself?
I ponder on God's greatness; He is God all by Himself!
I start to try and name the many things that He has done.
I try to count the many times, the victory He's won.

I try, but in my trying, I forget so many things.
Yet, in it all, though memory dim, I stand in awe of Him!

Sand on the Seashore

God said He's numbered every grain of sand on the seashore.
Have you ever stopped to wonder what a task He did endure?
Yes, everything's important, nothing escapes His eyes;
if He can take the time for 'sand', He certainly hears your cries!

One day I walked along the beach, on the sand so soft and white,
I took a handful of that sand and held it oh, so tight!
I tried to count each little grain, as I stood there by the sea;
it soon became so clear to me, "what an impossibility!"
And then I heard His voice say, "This lesson, child, please learn,
what is impossible with Man is possible with God!"

I do not question how, or why, or when, or where He did it,
I just believe what's in His Word, because the Bible says it.
And, sitting there that day I learned, who truly is "The Man".
I learned so many great things as the sand slipped through my hand.

I learned to trust what God has said.
I learned to stand up tall.
I learned that He does care for me,
though I am so very small.
I learned that nothing happens, of which He is unaware.
I learned that, yes, through thick and thin, He will 'always' be there!

Sitting by the Seaside

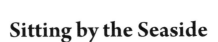

Sitting by the seaside, in the early morning dew,
it's such an awesome feeling to see a day so new!
The sun rising in the distance, is something to behold,
and just to think this day will bring so many tales untold!
The water splashes against the rocks, demanding my attention.
The angry waves move in and out in such form and dimension.
The world is still so quiet, in slumber and in sleep;
it's in this quite time alone, our God will sometimes speak.

Yes, to those angry waters, He can say "peace be still",
and they will very quickly rush, to obey His will.
Those solid rocks that's grounded way underneath the sea,
He only has to speak the 'Word', and they'll no longer be.
But the water is refreshing and it helps to make us clean,
and if those rocks were not in place, we'll have nowhere to lean.
Yes, everything that God does is in His 'perfect' plan,
and if we learn to trust Him, He will gently hold our hand.

God did not promise the waters won't beat against the rocks.
He did say He'll sustain us, and He'll always have our backs.
Yes, as the winds and waves persist, and we're tossed to and fro,
we may be tossed, we may be bruised, but He will not let us go!
No matter how the seas rage or the stormy billows blow,
it pays to have an anchor they cannot overthrow!
Yes, Jesus is that anchor, in Him there's peace and calm,
and when the storm is ended, we will emerge unharmed!

The Decision

Is it worth it when you've done all you can, to show someone you really care,
and they try their best to return your love, but the feeling just isn't there?
Over and over you've expressed the pain and the hurt this feeling has caused,
but all you get in return for your love, is a person who shows no remorse.

How much do you plan to go through, how much do you think you can take?
Eventually your nerves will give way, and your poor heart will finally break.
You will feel that you are the inferior one, and nothing you do will bring back,
the love that was lost when someone stepped in, and your world began to rock.

The emptiness, and the pain, it has caused, haunts you from day to day.
If only somehow you could understand, it does not have to remain that way.
Why do you feel you must bear all this pain; why do you feel you must stay?
There must be a better existence for you; there must be a better way.

You've tried, yes, God knows that you've tried, but it all seems to no avail,
because in your trying, you feel someone blocking the seas that you need to sail.
If there's an answer, ask God to let you now, ask Him if you're missing the mark,
for your world is so sad and lonely and dreary, and dismal and scary and dark.

Should you run to Papa and to Mama, and let them know how you feel,
Or should you go to your sister or brother, and let them know what's the deal?
Your Mama and Papa may cry and cry, or even get sick and die;
your sister and brother will look back at you, and point you to the sky.

This is your life and you have to live it, by doing what's best for you;
you must try to make some changes within it, and happiness somehow pursue.
You can start by putting your trust in the Lord, since no one else seems to care;
and even if someone does care for you, these burdens they cannot bear.

Then after all, has been said and done, and you've had many discussions,
it's right back again to one simple answer, just trust God for His decision.
Wait on the Lord, wait on the Lord, wait on Him patiently.
Trust and believe, and you will receive, a decision that fits 'perfectly'!

The Room

The room is filled with such nice things,
like curtains, made of lace.
There're lots of goodies for us to taste,
inside this pretty place.

But what really impresses me,
is the warmth I feel right now,
as people get together,
as they relate somehow.

This is what God intended,
this is what He wants for us!
For survival of the 'human race',
getting along is a 'must'!

The Struggle

With mixed feelings I struggle to get through another day,
knowing I don't have a choice, but to do it anyway.
I do, You say, do tell me what, and I will gladly look Your way,
in search of something that will take me through another day.
And at that moment on my knees, Dear God I start to pray,
please give me strength to make it through, just one day.

Today, I struggle hard, my Lord, just to do Your will;
wondering if I stumbled, would You love me still?
Then with much sorrow in my heart, I gently heard You whisper,
"By my blood you're made whole my child, for it heals any blister."
"All I ask for you to do, is to move on, I'll make you strong."
"Release it all to Me dear child, let your fears and tears be gone!"

"I knew you way before you were conceived, you are my child;
so, do not be deceived, I have been with you, all the while."
"When all you wanted to do was sit down and cry in pain,
I carried you when you were weak, until you were strong again!"
When storm clouds gather in the sky, and threatens to brings rain,
don't be afraid, all you have to do, is whisper, "Peace Be Still!"

Rejoicing

As I kneel here analyzing the whole thing,
I have no cares or worries is what You're saying. So,
why, I ask, am I so sad as I kneel praying?
Yes, I'll rise up and go on my way rejoicing!

Rejoicing just because you are my king!
Rejoicing because I don't need anything!
Rejoicing that one day, you'll burst the clouds, and
all your people will shout out aloud…

All hail King Jesus, The King of glory on His throne,
yes, He has come to take His children home!!

The Water's Edge

The waves come in against the shore, as I walk towards the sea;
they seem to be inviting me to enter, naturally.
"The water's cold", *I* tell myself. "You dare not step into it",
but as I approach the water's edge, my mind says, "You go for it!"

I'll dive right in; no other way would be appropriate;
to try and ease myself in would only decrease my faith.
So, in I go, I take the plunge, knowing I could not wait;
I cannot help but think, "That's what God wants, by faith!"

My body trembles for a while, and then at last, I'm fine;
to make me leave the water now, would almost be a crime!

The Wonder of God's Love

God's love, so wonderful; a thing of beauty,
all put together with such love divine!
The joys, the blessings we receive from one so loving,
to those who will accept Him as their friend and guide!
His faithfulness surpasses all expectations,
and goes beyond our wildest imaginations!

Oh, if we would only stop to realize,
just how much He truly loved mankind!
Willing to make the total sacrifice;
giving His life, to redeem us from all sin and strife!
If man would serve Him, and be faithful to the end,
I guarantee He'll be your constant friend!

He'll bring us out of any sin that holds us bondage,
and out of trials and tribulations too.
He'll break all the bad habits and addictions;
He'll break the strongholds that's destroying you!
Yes, God will save you from your own destruction,
and gently point you in the right direction!

Come humbly to Him, come and bow before Him.
Come confessing you have truly sinned.
He'll be waiting with open arms to meet you,
and usher you to gladly enter in.
To a place of peace and comfort He will lead you,
just trust him, He'll be there to see you through!

The Word

The 'Word' says, **whosoever** will, may come,
and He'll accept us as we are.
The 'Word' says all we like sheep has gone astray,
and has turned everyone to his own way,
but loving us so much God give His only son, that
whosoever
believe on Him, shall not perish,
but have everlasting life.
God's Word is true! God's Word is sure!
God's Word shall stand forevermore!

View from My Window

From my window I can feel like, the world is watching me;
the land, the sea, the grass the trees, in sweet serenity!
Then my mind starts to wonder, and I can't help but ponder,
there must be a God, He must be Lord, in all His royal splendor!

The great creator of all this, my mind cannot dismiss;
He made the sun the moon, the stars, they do not just exist!
He took His time and made, all the things on His list,
He made them to His liking, it was no hit-or-miss!

Then came the greatest of them all, in His creation plan!
God took the dirt we walk on, and He created man!
He molded him and formed him, it was His 'perfect' plan,
he then made a woman, from the rib of that 'perfect' man!

Man failed, to do God's bidding, he was in a broken state;
God knew man must come back to Him, so they could both relate!
God had a plan, He'd put in place, since He knew it from the start;
He sent His son, His only son, to die and change man's heart!

So, today I am so thankful, as from my window I observe,
I know the world is watching me, my place God has reserved.
I have no care, or worry, I'll just enjoy the view,
and if you care to join me, you are 'very' welcome to!

Who Else Can I Trust?

Who else can I trust, if I can't trust you Lord?
What else can I believe in, if not in your Word?
You've been there for me in ways I can't see;
Lord I trust You, to take care of me.

Who else can I trust when the doctors don't know?
Who else can I trust; Lord I depend on you so.
I trust you to guide me, when my way I can't see;
I know I can trust you to be there with me.

Who else can I trust when finances are low?
You own everything, yes, your 'Word' tells me so.
So, I'll trust you no matter how dark the outlook;
I believe in the words of your Holy Book!

Who else will I trust when life's end seems so close?
I'll continue to trust you, for me you died and arose.
And when this life is over; if in you I abide,
I will live with you forever, on the other side!

You Know

You know the hurt; you know the pain.
You know the guilt; you know the shame...
Lord you know.

You know the times I tried and I failed.
You know I've tried and tried again...
Lord you know.

You know you've brought me to this place;
a future without you I cannot face...
Lord you know.

You know I need you in my space.
You know I need your saving grace...
Lord you know.

And so today on bending knees,
I ask forgiveness would you please?
Lord let me feel your presence near;
Please help me know that you are here.

Lord welcome me with open arms,
Your loving kindness my spirit calms.
Forgive me Lord for I have sinned;
I open up, please enter in.

Yes, enter in this open door,
and live within forever more!

Hope you enjoyed the stroll!
Please return soon, and invite
your friends...